Above *Large, white ceramic tiles complete this modern kitchen. They provide a practical flooring surface. The choice of white as a colour, and the positioning of the island unit in the centre of the tiled area, gives a clean, efficient look to the room.*

Left *The pale green of the stained glass has been echoed in the tiles in this tiny bathroom. To avoid a feeling of claustrophobia, all paintwork, fittings, towels, etc. have been kept either white or pale pink.*

TOOLS AND MATERIALS

Here is a list of the tools and materials you will find mentioned later in the book.

Spirit level: An accurate level is a must for planning the layout (setting out) tiles on walls and determining the slope of floors.

Chalk line is a reel of non-stretch string that is used to make straight lines on walls, floors and ceilings.

To 'snap' a chalk line, fasten one end to a nail (or get a helper to hold it) on one mark, and hold it taut to the second mark. Then pull the line away from the surface and let it snap back. There will be a straight line of chalk between the two marks.

Plumb line is a string with a weight on the end that, hanging free, shows a true vertical. It can be rubbed with chalk and used as above.

Battens are lengths of softwood used in setting out wall and floor tiles. Choose straight ones of about 50mm × 25mm (unless a specific size is stated).

Gauge stick is a setting out tool you make yourself. Lay out a row of tiles, being sure to space them as they will be when fixed. Simply butt self-spacing tiles together. Then place a batten next to the tiles and mark it at the corner of each tile. Use the gauge stick by placing it against the wall or floor to find the best position for the rows of tiles.

Scriber is used to set out floor tiles. It is easy to make yourself, as it is simply a batten approximately 1 metre long with a nail driven through both ends, so that the points protrude. (See page 22.)

Tile cutters: There are several types of proprietary tile cutters. The most common resembles pliers with two 'wings' and also a wheel used to score the tile. The jaws are used to snap the tile on the line.

For cutting floor tiles, it's best to hire a steel tile cutter. It'll cost more, but save on shattered tiles.

Adhesive spreaders are plastic or metal trowels with notches on the edge. They apply adhesive in even ridges and so help to avoid thick and thin patches. Often they're supplied free with the adhesive.

Float is a rectangular metal or wooden plate with a handle on the top. It is used for spreading screed or laying sand and cement mortar on floors.

Tile spike is a traditional tool for scoring the line where a tile is to be cut. This creates a weak point, making it possible to break the tile along the line.

Tile nibblers are pincers that are used to break off small pieces of tile, 'nibbling' away the waste on an awkward shape.

Tile breaking board: A flat piece of wood is helpful for snapping the tiles once they're scored.

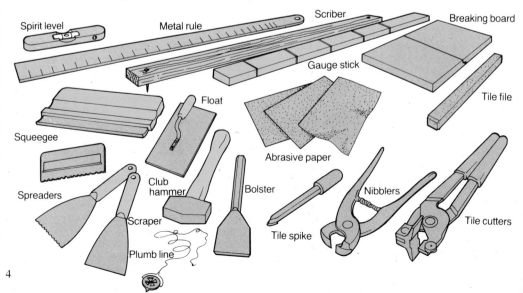

Spirit level · Metal rule · Scriber · Breaking board · Gauge stick · Tile file · Float · Squeegee · Abrasive paper · Spreaders · Club hammer · Bolster · Nibblers · Scraper · Tile spike · Tile cutters · Plumb line

TILE IT

Dek Messecar
Series Consultant Editor: Bob Tattersall

CONTENTS

Introduction	2
Tools and Materials Basic Tools, Adhesives and Grouts. Types of Ceramic Tiles	4
Wall Tiles Ceramic Tiles and Mosaics, Plastic, Metal, Mirror and Cork Tiles Preparing Walls Setting Out Fixing, Cutting and Grouting	6
Ceiling Tiles	17
Floor Tiles Ceramic, Cork, Vinyl, Rubber and Carpet Tiles Preparing Floors Setting Out Fixing, Cutting and Grouting	18
Special Effects Ideas for using tiles	28
Top Ten Tips	30
Safety Tips	31
Credits	32

COLLINS

Introduction

The use of clay tiles to protect and decorate walls and floors is as old as brick making and pottery, and certainly precedes the invention of paint and even paper.

The advantage of being able to manufacture and decorate each small piece separately before applying it eliminates problems in construction (such as expansion) and offers many possibilities for design.

Today, most decorating materials are available in tile form. As well as the vast ranges of ceramic tiles, there are mirrored glass, cork, plastics, aluminium, stainless steel, vinyl, rubber and carpet.

Tiling techniques are the same for all materials except for the methods of cutting them and adhesives for fixing them. Tiles are easier to handle than sheet materials, and actually fixing them to walls and floors is simple. The one problem is that the first tile determines the position of every other. This is where do-it-yourself tiling jobs can be spoiled before they begin. The secret is to plan the entire job before fixing that first tile. This is called 'setting out'.

The main area of the wall or floor is called the 'field' and is always tiled first with whole, uncut tiles. This leaves the spaces around the edges, called the 'border', to be tiled seperately, each tile being cut to fit. A well-done job has a balanced appearance, as though the tiles fell into place quite naturally and without effort. However, this is the result of spending as much time setting out the job as in fixing the tiles.

This book will help you to do a good job. It will also help you to choose the right tile for the project you have in mind, and there are lots of colour photographs to set you thinking about that next project.

Above *Antique tiles are often to be found in second-hand shops and on market stalls. They can be attractively used either in sets, or by matching-up a number of odd tiles by colour, design, size, etc.*

Left *Large unglazed quarry tiles are a perfect foil for the renovated cafe table which serves as a home office area in this country style kitchen.*

You can place matchsticks under the line at each edge, or for better results, fix a piece of bare wire across it. This supports the full width of the tile, giving a better chance of breaking it on the line.

Straight edge: A metal rule or straight strip of metal is necessary for guiding the tile spike (or cutter wheel) or the trimming knife.

Tile file: The best tool for smoothing the cut edges of ceramic tiles is a carborundum file, made of the same material as a knife sharpening stone. In fact, a stone can be used, although it's not as good for getting into small places.

Rubber squeegee: To spread grout over the tiles and into the joints, use a thin rubber wiper with a handle of the kind used to clean windows. It's quicker than a sponge.

Filling knife and scraper: These look similar, but have different functions. The scraper is stiff and is used to remove wallpaper and flaking paint. The filling knife is flexible and is used to apply filler to cracks and holes in walls and ceilings.

Bonding agent: When sealing cement floors or to help new cement to bond to old, you should use a polyvinyl acetate adhesive diluted with water.

Self-levelling compound screed is a water- or resin-based compound that is mixed to a creamy consistency and poured over slightly uneven floors. It doesn't require skill in smoothing the surface because it finds its own level and flattens out.

Adhesives: Don't try using the wrong tile adhesive for the job. They are designed for specific purposes. The manufacturers always state which one to use for walls and which for floors. Also, you must use a flexible adhesive whenever tiling a surface that may have some movement, such as chipboard, hardboard or plywood sheets.

There are frost-proof adhesives for use outside and heat-resistant ones for work surfaces and fire places, and for surfaces that are often under water, such as shower floors, you must use a waterproof adhesive.

Contact adhesive: If the manufacturer recommends fixing cork tiles with contact adhesive, use a water-based (rather than solvent-based) one. These are much easier to apply and have no heavy, infammable fumes.

Grout: As with adhesives, the material in the joints between the tiles must be flexible, frost-proof, heat-resistant, or waterproof as the situation demands. Also, on tiled work surfaces where food is prepared, use a non-toxic grout.

Filler for surface repairs comes in powder form to be mixed with water, or ready to use. Modern resin-based fillers are better than cellulose filler as they dry without shrinking, so cracks and holes can be filled flush.

Silicone caulk: Available in tubes and in various colours, this mastic makes a water-tight seal between bath tubs and basins and the tiles. It remains flexible enough to accommodate movement. It also provides a good way of sealing the join between floor tiles and wall tiles.

Chemical wallpaper stripper is a jelly-like product that clings to the surface of old wallpaper and can be used instead of water and vinegar when following the soak and scrape method. (See page 9.)

Spacing the tiles

A space has to be left between tiles to allow for movement due to humidity and temperature changes. This space is filled with grout to stop dirt from collecting in it and must be the same size throughout otherwise the finished result will look odd.

Accuracy of spacing is easy with modern Universal tiles. These are bevelled on each edge so that you can butt the tiles closely to each other, leaving a V-shaped gap that allows for expansion and can be filled with grout in the normal way.

The bevel also allows Universals to be used at the top and sides of a panel without the need for special edging tiles.

Square-edged tiles often have spacer lugs on each edge and are known as self-spacing tiles. Butt the lugs closely together and you are assured of uniform spacing.

If you are using neither Universal nor self-spacing tiles, you can buy plastic tile spacers (or use matchsticks) which will ensure an even result.

WALL TILES

Tiling a complete wall with mirror tiles has the effect of making the room seem twice the size.

Ceramic tiles for use on walls are available from many scources in vast ranges of colours, designs and sizes. Surfaces may be as smooth as glass or textured and matt. In fact the surface of glazed tiles is glass, making them a practical, hardwearing surface.

As well as different finishes, tiles may have different properties according to the use for which they're meant. Some tiles are heat-resistant while others are frost-proof.

Modern ceramic tiles have lugs on the edges to take the effort out of keeping them uniformly spaced. Square tiles with unfinished edges are called 'field tiles'. However, where tiles meet on external corners, there are special tiles that are used to finish the edges. The traditional tiles for this are called 'round-edge (RE), which has a rounded finished edge, and 'double round-edge' (REX) with two adjacent finished edges. These tiles are laid to cover the edges of the field tiles.

To finish the edge of field tiles on a flat surface, such as the top row of a half-tiled wall, there are 'quadrant tiles'. These are like a narrow strip of a round-edge tile. They can help give an authentic look to traditional patterns and antique tiles.

Another type of edge finishing tile is sometimes called a 'universal tile'. These usually have two glazed edges.

Mosaics are supplied in sheets of equally spaced pieces (known as chips), making them as easy to fix as tiles.

Just as there is a choice of types of tiles, so tile adhesives and grouts are also made for different purposes. See the 'Tools and Materials' pages to make sure you buy the right one for the job and always follow the manufacturers' instructions.

Plastic tiles are made from thin plastic sheet to imitate ceramic wall tiles. Although they aren't as strong as ceramic tiles, their surface is warmer and they are very easy to fix, usually with self-adhesive pads. Their main disadvantage is that they cannot withstand heat, so don't use them near cookers or fireplaces.

This room leads off a covered patio area. Random use of picture tiles helps soften the otherwise rather cold effect.

Different coloured cork tiles have been used to add a touch of design to what is a practical and economic finish.

Cork, rubber, vinyl and carpet tiles may be used on walls, although cork is the most usual. The attraction of these materials, apart from their appearance, is that they are warm to the touch and also help to reduce noise by absorbing, rather than reflecting, it. The advantage of using them in tile form is that waste is kept to a minimum.

Cork is available in different qualities for floors and walls. The floor tiles are compressed to increase their density. Wall tiles come in different thicknesses and densities. Unfinished cork can be finished with two coats of clear polyurethane or (on walls) left natural.

Cork tiles are available in various natural shades and some tiles have a slight grain direction that can be used to create a pattern.

Metal tiles are fixed with pads in the same way as plastic ones. They are usually fixed butted together (without grouting) and provide a heat-resistant and washable surface, although splash marks must be cleaned off regularly.

The aluminium ones usually cut easily with scissors, but you may need tin snips for stainless steel tiles.

A major feature of metal tiles is that they can be bent around internal and external corners.

Mirror tiles are simply mirrored glass cut into tiles. The most important thing to remember is that the surface to which they are fixed must be absolutely flat and smooth. Any unevenness will cause a distorted reflection. One way to overcome this is by fixing plywood or chipboard to the wall.

As mirror tiles are butted together without grout, it's a good idea to lay them out first on a flat surface. They may not all be exactly square and there can be some variation in size.

With all tiles, the quality of the job is decided at the planning stage. It takes as long to find the best arrangement, both for working out a pattern and to give the overall job a professional symmetry, as to actually fix the tiles.

Preparing Walls

Plaster

New plaster needs at least one month to dry out before it can be tiled. Remove any little splashes (small bumps) of plaster and fill any cracks or dents. Then prime with a plaster primer or any universal primer to create a non-absorbent surface for the tile adhesive.

Filling cracks and dents

This is done with the flexible filling knife and filler described in 'Tools and Materials'.

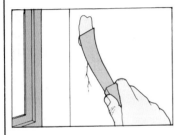

Scoop some filler on to the end of the knife and press the blade flat over the fault, sliding away to leave the filler in the hole. You may need several attempts to ensure the filler is pushed right to the bottom without air being trapped underneath (if the filler bulges out of the hole there's an air bubble under it).

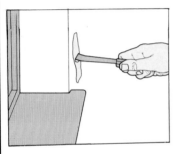

When you've applied enough to fill the hole, hold the knife almost vertically and scrape across the top to remove the excess.

Professionals try to clean all the surplus away (including the ridges around the edges) leaving the repair flush. It's worth the extra time spent on the wet filler as rubbing down afterwards is messy, time consuming and hard work.

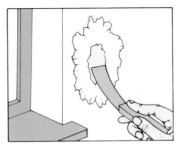

Large, deep holes should be filled in layers not more than 3mm thick. These dry quickly enough that you can apply a layer every so often while dealing with other small repairs.

Filling with thin layers helps with faults that are wider than the filling knife. The surface is built up gradually around the edges, reducing the area to be scraped off flush. Remember to clean the surplus from around the edges each time you fill.

Very large areas of damaged plaster should be repaired with plaster or one of the DIY plastering systems that is applied by brush. These are used in layers up to 3mm thick and take 24 hours to dry between coats so, if the fault is deeper than this, use ordinary filler to build up the surface until only a 'skim coat' is needed. Keep working the surface (re-wetting if necessary) until you're satisfied with the finish.

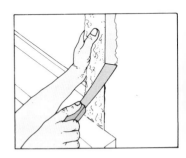

To get a neat edge on outside corners, hold a polythene-wrapped piece of wood against one side and flush with the edge. Fill the gap as if it were a crack. Then slide the wood away when the filler begins to set. Use a damp sponge to remove traces of wet filler.

Wallpaper

Wallpaper or other wall coverings cannot be tiled. It is necessary to strip off all layers of old paper to reveal the plaster. Do this either by the 'soak and scrape method' as described below, or use a steam stripper, widely available from hire shops and easy to use.

Removing wallpaper

First, check whether the paper is of the 'peel off' variety by grasping a corner and pulling. Vinyl types are easily removed like this, but they leave their paper backing on the wall. This must be removed in the normal way.

To remove other wallpapers, begin by scoring the surface with a stiff wire brush. This is particularly important with washable (i.e. water-resistant) papers and those that have been painted over.

Next, fill a bucket with warm water and add a little vinegar (this reduces the surface tension and helps it to penetrate the paper). Using a large paint or pasting brush, soak the paper as much as possible.

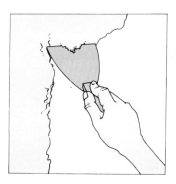

Use a stiff scraping knife to get under the paper, but be careful

not to dig into the surface of the plaster. Keep re-soaking until the paper comes off easily, leaving little residue. After stripping, wash off any traces of old adhesive with clean water.

For stubborn papers, try one of the *chemical wallpaper stripping products* instead of water and vinegar. These cling to the surface and allow more time for the adhesive to soften.

Painted walls

Gloss paint must be rubbed down with medium grade abrasive paper to key the adhesive. Matt finish paint needs to be washed and rinsed. Use a scraper to remove any loose paint and then fill as plaster. Remember to prime any bare areas or filler.

Old ceramic tiles

Existing tiles may be tiled over if they are firmly stuck and any cracks filled. If the old tiles are glazed, rub them down with a coarse grade silicon carbide paper to scratch the surface slightly. This will help 'key' the surface for the adhesive. Then wipe the surface with a cloth dampened with white spirit to remove any dust and old polish.

Brick or rough concrete

Uneven masonry walls will have to be plastered or rendered or lined with chipboard or plywood.

Wood

Timber has always been considered a problem surface for tiles because, as the timber moves with changes in temperature and humidity, the tiles will be pulled in different directions, causing cracks to

appear. However, modern adhesives have overcome this problem. Now you can tile on wood, but you must make sure you use the correct adhesive.

How to line walls

To make a smooth, stable surface for tiling, you can fix plywood or chipboard (particle board) sheets to battens.

Screw battens to the wall not more than 30cm apart. Fix the first one at the corner. Using the width of the sheets, calculate the other battens to be spaced equally, with a batten at the join with the next sheet. The last sheet on the wall will probably need to be cut to fit.

If there is a window or door, fix battens around the edges. Cut the sheets to fit the area to be tiled.

Use a long, straight piece of wood to keep the battens straight and parallel with each other. If necessary, use pieces of wood to space some battens away from the wall.

When all the battens are up, mark their positions on the sheets and screw the sheets to the battens. Prime the wood with an oil-based primer to create a non-absorbent surface and to prevent rust on the screw heads.

Fixing Wall Tiles

First, choose the most important wall or surface. Decide this according either to how prominently it is featured, or how many awkward corners and obstacles are on it. The tiles on any adjoining walls will have to follow suit.

On a plain wall without obstacles, the tiles should be fixed so that the cut border tiles are of equal size on each side and top and bottom. Also, the border tiles should not be less than half a tile width. If, when setting out, there are spaces at the ends of the vertical or horizontal rows that are narrower than this, reduce the number of whole tiles in the row by one.

It is difficult to cut thin strips (less than 25mm) of ceramic tiles and narrow 'L' shapes are fragile and unsightly. The final result will depend most on how carefully you can arrange to have the fewest problem border spaces to fill, and on placing them where they won't be noticed.

Having chosen your tiles, make a gauge stick of a convenient length for the job.

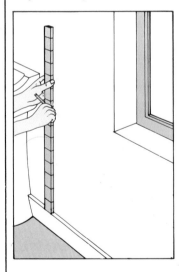

If you're tiling *floor to ceiling*, hold the stick vertically to find the best arrangement for the *horizontal rows*, marking the wall with a pencil where the joins will be. Use trial and error to balance the top and bottom rows of cut tiles equally.

If there is a sink or bath, it's better to have a row of whole tiles along the top of it. On the other hand, if there is a window, it is usually best to treat it as the focal point, and centre the rows of tiles on this.

When you think you've found the best arrangement, mark the wall where the bottom of the lowest row of whole tiles will be.

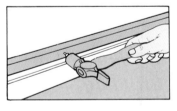

Cut a length of batten to fit the wall and drive nails into it every 30cm or so. Hold the batten on the mark and drive the first nail. Then, using the spirit level to get it perfectly horizontal, drive the remaining nails far enough into the wall to hold the batten firmly, but not all the way in. This makes it easier to remove the batten later.

Rest the gauge stick vertically on the batten at different points along the wall to see how doors, windows, sinks, etc. will be affected.

Now you should be able to decide which feature or obstacle is the most important and what compromise will be best for the others. If necessary move the batten.

If you're *half-tiling*, and want to use a number of rows of whole tiles, use a tile and a pencil to mark the wall (or walls) along the skirting board. Cut a batten to fit the wall and drive nails into it every 30cm or so.

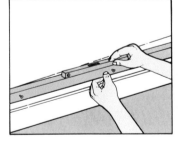

Hold the batten against the wall and use the spirit level to adjust it level with the lowest point of the line. This makes sure there will be no gap below the bottom row of tiles, although it may be necessary to cut some of them if the skirting board isn't level. Drive the nails into the wall far enough to hold the batten, but not fully home.

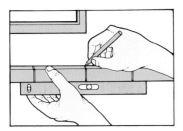

Now you can use the gauge stick to plan the *vertical rows.* Hold a spirit level and the gauge stick in one hand to keep it approximately level and mark the joins on the wall with a pencil.

Treat windows and other obstacles as for horizontal rows or allow equal size cut tiles at either side of the wall.

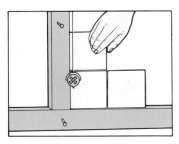

Once you are satisfied with the setting out of the vertical rows, nail a batten either at the central join or at the last row of full tiles on one side of the wall. Use the spirit level or a plumb line to make sure it's perfectly vertical.

It's a good idea to try holding a number of tiles without adhesive in the corner between the battens to make sure they are at right angles to each other.

Fixing ceramic wall tiles

Now you are ready to begin fixing the tiles. All the whole tiles will be fixed first. The cut tiles are left until the adhesive under the whole tiles has hardened.

Follow the manufacturers' instructions in mixing or stirring the adhesive and have the spreader, a damp sponge, and a supply of matchsticks (if the tiles don't have spacer lugs).

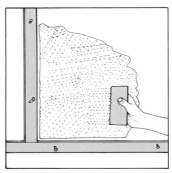

Begin by spreading approximately 1 square metre of adhesive where the battens meet. Make sure the wall is covered up to, but not touching, the battens.

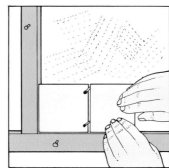

Starting with the bottom row, press the tiles, without sliding them, firmly into the adhesive. Push self spacing tiles together

so the lugs are touching. Insert matchsticks between tiles that have no lugs.

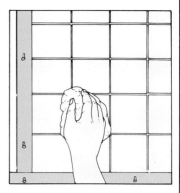

Continue tiling until the area of adhesive is covered. Wipe off any adhesive that squeezes on to the surface of the tiles with a damp sponge.

Then spread another area and continue along the bottom. After every three or four horizontal rows, hold a batten and spirit level along the top of the tiles to make sure they're horizontal.

When you come to a place where the bottom row of whole tiles will be higher, such as above a basin, bath, or window nail up a short batten (using the spirit level) to keep them from slipping down before the adhesive sets.

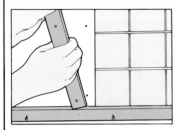

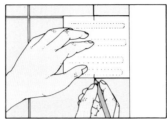

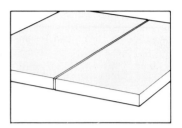

If the vertical batten is in the centre of the wall, remove it carefully to tile the rest of the wall.

Finish fixing all the whole tiles and then remove any adhesive from the space around the edges, which would interfere with fixing the cut tiles later.

Allow the adhesive to set before taking down the bottom battens.

How to cut tiles

Now you are ready to fill the remaining spaces. All the cut tiles are to be fixed so that the 'factory edge' is next to another tile, and the cut edge against an adjacent wall or fitting.

You will need: a tile spike and breaking board or a proprietary tile cutter, a metal straight edge, pencil or chinagraph pencil, tape measure, tile nibblers and tile file.

If you have a long row of straight cut tiles to fix, you can cut and fix one at a time, or cut all of them first and then fix them. If you do cut them all first, number the spaces on the wall and the back of each tile so you known which one fits where.

Here is a method of measuring that ensures the tile will fit even if the width at the top and bottom of the tile is different (against a sloping wall, for instance).

Hold a tile with its face to the wall and mark the edge at the top and bottom where the uncut edge will be. Allow space for the join with the fixed tile and also for a small gap with the other wall.

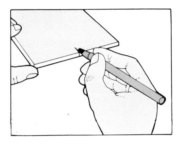

Looking at the edge of the tile, transfer these marks to the face side. If the tiles are glazed, use a chinagraph pencil to make the marks clear.

Place the tile on a piece of wood and use a straight edge and tile cutter to score a line across the face.

The depth of the scored line is not as important as how sharp the bottom is. It is better to make one confident, smooth cut than to scratch several times with too much force. You must score right around the edges of the tile to make sure there will be a clean break.

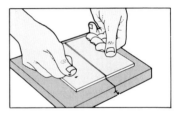

Place the tile on a breaking board with the line directly over the wire or ridge (or place a matchstick under the line at each edge) and snap it by pushing down on both sides equally.

Alternatively, you can use the edge of a table. Hold one side firmly and snap off the other side.

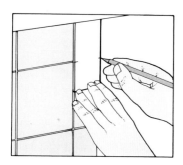

To measure the corner tile in the row, hold it up once for the width and cut, and then repeat the operation for the height.

The easiest way to measure an odd-shape cut is to make a paper template the same size as a tile, and make cuts in it so that each flap can be folded to the shape of the obstruction.

Place the template on the tile and mark and score the shape.

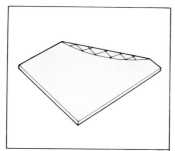

Score a line to remove as much of the waste as you can, and then score a grid of lines, being careful to keep them on the waste side of the line.

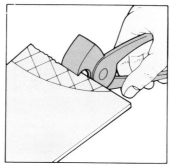

Use the tile nibblers to break off small pieces until the line is reached. Then, if necessary, smooth the cut edge with a file.

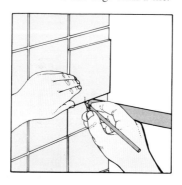

Where you must fit a tile around a pipe, mark where the

pipe will be on the tile by measuring from the adjacent tiles.

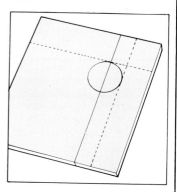

Score around the edge of a coin or other round object that is a little larger than the pipe, and also score a straight line across the tile through the circle.

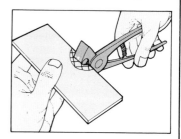

Snap the tile along the straight line, and then nibble out the semi-circle on each piece.

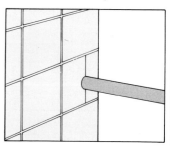

When the pieces are fixed, the join will hardly show.

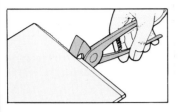

When you have to cut a small strip from a tile (perhaps when trimming the bottom row of tiles), score it in the normal way, and use the nibblers rather than snapping it.

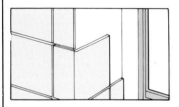

On the inside of a window reveal, fix whole tiles so that they overlap the edges of the tiles on the wall. Make sure the joins match the wall tiles and cut the end ones as necessary. Then fix cut tiles between the frame and the whole tiles.

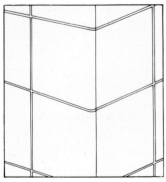

On other outside corners, the finished edge tiles on the more important surface should cover the edges of the tiles on the other.

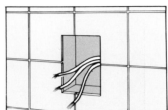

To tile round a light switch or power socket, first switch off the electricity at the mains. Then remove the cover and cut tiles to fit around the box. After replacing the cover, you can restore the electricity.

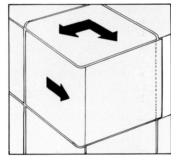

When you come to tile three surfaces (such as a boxed-in basin), the tile on the top should overlap the edges of those on the sides. To keep the joins matching between the top and the sides, one of the tiles on the corner will have to be cut.

When tiling the panel at the side of a bathtub, remember to make a removable section for access to the plumbing. This can be held in place with a hinge and magnetic catches. Be sure to use flexible adhesive on panels and don't grout the joins at the edges.

Grouting

When all the tiles have been fixed, leave the adhesive to harden for the time recommended by the manufacturer (usually 24 hours). The next job is to fill the joins between the tiles with a suitable grout – see 'Tools and Materials'.

If you have tiled around a bath or sink, first use a silicone caulk between these and the tiles. Grout can become discoloured here and also the movement may cause it to crack. Allow the caulk to harden before grouting the wall.

Mix the grout, adding colour if desired, following the manufacturers' instructions. You will also need a rubber squeegee, a bucket of clean water, and a flat sponge.

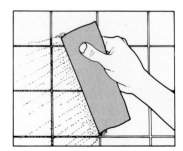

Spread the grout liberally over the joints, pushing it well in. Use the squeegee or sponge diagonally to move the excess along to the next area.

Use a flat sponge to wipe most of the grout from the face of the tiles before it sets. Rinse the sponge frequently in the clean water (rinsing under the tap can silt up the drain).

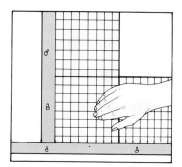

As the grout begins to harden, use a stick with a rounded tip along the joints to give a neat finish.

When the grout has set, remove the excess grout with a damp sponge, rinsed often in clean water. Then remove the last film of grout by polishing the tiles with a soft cloth.

Fixing mosaics

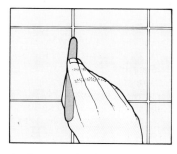

Set out the job in the same way as for normal ceramic tiles, treating each sheet as a whole tile. Set up vertical and horizontal battens. If there is a protective paper covering on the face of the sheets, leave it on until they're fixed and dry.

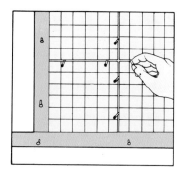

Fix 3 or 4 sheets at a time. Use spacers to make the gaps between the sheets the same as the gap between each tile on the sheet, unless the manufacturers' instructions say to butt them together.

If there are arrows on the back of the sheets, make sure they all point the same way. When all the whole sheets have been fixed, leave them to dry.

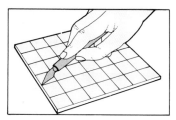

Cut off enough rows to more than fill the space.

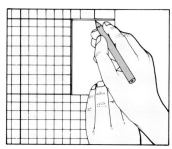

Place the partial sheet face to the wall and mark the edges.

Use the spacer card against the wall to make the correct gap between sheets.

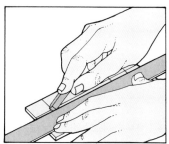

Place the sheet face up on a piece of wood and score the line across all the tiles.

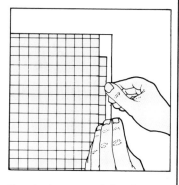

Cut the last row of tiles from the sheet and spread adhesive in the space to be filled. Fix the partial sheet.

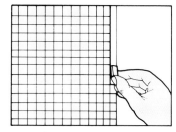

Break the individual tiles with the tile cutter, fixing each one as you go to prevent them getting mixed up.

Plastic tiles

Setting out is done as for ceramic tiles, but don't worry about intricate cutting as the plastic can be easily cut with scissors.

The back of each tile is hollow. It is fixed to the wall by placing self adhesive foam pads on the corners and, usually, one in the middle.

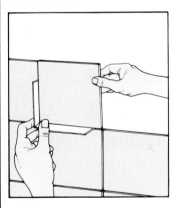

Peel the backing paper off the pads and press the tiles firmly in position, spacing with a card if necessary. The pads grip immediately, so you won't be able to adjust the tiles. Fix the whole tiles first, then fill in the borders.

Follow the manufacturers' instructions for grouting.

Metal foil tiles

These are fixed with pads in the same way as plastic tiles, except that the edges are butted close together.

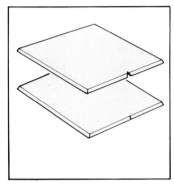

To bend them around corners, snip the bevelled or curved edges as far as the flat area for internal corners, or remove a wedge shaped piece for external corners. Start with a thin wedge and use trial and error to find the best shape.

Bend the tile to the required angle over a sharp edged piece of wood.

Mirror tiles

These are fixed either in the same way as plastic and metal tiles, or with a special adhesive specified by the manufacturer.

Mirror tiles are cut in the same way as ceramic wall tiles. Use a glass cutter to score the line and then snap it over a sharp edge. Intricate cuts are extremely difficult so it may be best to confine these tiles to an area without problems.

Cork tiles

Setting out for cork tiles is the same as for ceramic wall tiles. Cork is much easier to cut so awkward border tiles are less of a problem. Cork tiles are best set out with equal space borders (side to side and top to bottom) of not less than $\frac{1}{2}$ a tile width.

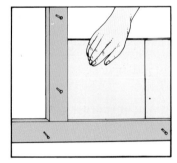

Fix a horizontal batten as for ceramic tiles. Then either fix a vertical batten at the centre join or use a chalked plumb line to snap a vertical line as described in 'Tools and Materials'.

For instructions for fixing cork (and other soft tiles) see the 'Floors' section.

SAFETY WARNING
Metal conducts electricity, so trim tiles around switch and socket covers. Don't remove the covers and insert tiles behind them.

Ceiling Tiles

Although any tiles can be used on the ceiling, expanded polystyrene tiles are more usual. Polystyrene tiles are the least expensive covering for a ceiling, apart from paint, and are available in a wide range of designs and patterns. There are also covings to be used around the edges of the ceiling to simulate plaster and tidy the joins between ceiling and walls.

Preparation is the same as for walls, but hairline cracks and small holes can be left. The main consideration is that the surface is sound and flat. Contours in the ceiling will cause the tiles to adopt crazy angles and look very untidy.

To avoid fire hazard, polystyrene tiles must be fixed with no air gaps behind them. Use the adhesive specified by the manufacturer and spread it over the whole tile. Don't use blobs of adhesive on each corner. Beware of using them on low ceilings over cookers or around metal chimneys that pass through the ceiling. Also you must not paint the tiles with oil-based paint; this also constitutes a fire risk. Only water-based emulsion paints are suitable.

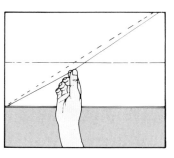

Set out the tiles to suit the most important wall or feature in the room in the same way as floor tiles. Snap the two chalk lines at right angles to each other.

Mix up the adhesive according to the manufacturers' instructions and spread it on the back of the first tile. To prevent it squeezing out between the tiles, it's best not to brush it quite to the edges.

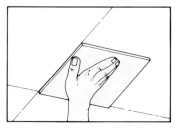

Place the tile in position where the chalk lines intersect and press it with the flat of your hand onto the ceiling to make sure it sticks all over. Don't use fingertips on polystyrene tiles or the surface may be dented.

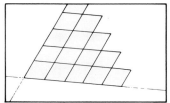

Work outward along the lines from the first tile, filling in the middle spaces. As polystyrene tiles are not exactly regular, leave a tiny (1mm) gap between them.

To help keep the rows straight, stand back every so often and sight down the joins. Fix all the whole tiles.

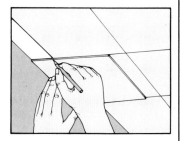

When only the border spaces remain, hold a tile upside down with its edge against the wall and mark the edges where it overlaps the last tile. Use a knife or a felt tip pen to nick the edge.

Place the tile face up on a piece of wood and use a metal straight edge and sharp knife to cut a line between the two marks. Make several passes with the blade at a low angle, as the beads of polystyrene sometimes tear out, leaving a ragged edge. A curved blade helps to make a cleaner cut.

You can use the methods described for measuring and cutting soft floor tiles (page 27) for any awkward edges.

FLOOR TILES

Ceramic floor tiles are the longest lasting floorcovering you can use. They are thicker than tiles made for walls, and also fired at so high a temperature (vitrified) that the particles of clay fuse together. This makes them almost unbreakable when laid, but it can also cause problems with cutting them to fit.

Traditional quarry tiles in natural earth colours are still available, but there are also huge ranges of designs and colours in modern, self-spacing versions. Most ranges of tiles include RE and REX tiles, and there are also covings that can be used, in place of skirting boards, around the edge of the tiled floor.

As floor tiles are much stronger than wall tiles, they are the best choice for work surfaces, hearths and window sills etc. Unglazed floor tiles will withstand the heat of a hot roasting pan without damage. However, if you use glazed tiles on a surface where food is prepared, make sure the glaze doesn't contain lead. Also, you must use heat-resistant adhesive and a non-toxic grout.

The first thing to consider is how much you can raise the level of your floor without causing too much other work. Doors can be taken off and trimmed quite easily, but check cupboard doors, too, and have a look at washing machines or dish washers that fit under the work surface.

There are two methods of laying ceramic floor tiles. You can use a thin layer (3 or 4mm) of adhesive or lay the tiles on a sand and cement screed at least 12mm thick. How to do this is described on the following pages.

If you are tiling an outside patio, path, or balcony, you may use either method, but be sure to use frost-proof tiles and adhesive.

Above *Provencal quarry tiles are very attractive, either inside or outside. These are unglazed, and being a non-porous tile should not stain easily. In a kitchen, however, it might be advisable to use a glazed version.*

Left *These glazed quarry tiles have been carried over the threshold to the patio, so pulling the two areas together and making both seem larger.*

Cork, vinyl, rubber and carpet floor tiles have the advantages of being comfortable and quiet to walk on and also easier to lay. However, they require a smooth and flat subfloor if they are to last well, so preparation is all important.

Cork floor tiles are compressed to increase their density. As with wall tiles, they are available with their surface already sealed by the manufacturer or left natural. In the case of floors, they must be sealed with at least two coats of polyurethane varnish or whatever the manufacturer recommends.

Vinyl coated tiles are one 'of the least expensive floor coverings and are much easier to use than in sheet form. Also, some tiles are self adhesive.

Solid vinyl tiles are expensive, but very hard wearing. They are available in wide ranges of colours and designs, some imitating marble, stone, wood etc.

Synthetic rubber tiles aren't cheap but they will last. They are very comfortable and quiet to walk on and the studded versions are popular for their 'high tech' look. However, colour ranges are limited when compared with ceramic and vinyl tiles.

Carpet tiles are sold in most qualities from inexpensive cords to heavy duty contract types and plush velvet piles. The advantage of tiles is minimum waste in fitting and also being able to replace a few worn tiles (or move them to a part of the floor that doesn't show) without replacing all of the carpeted area. Using different colours of carpet tiles to create patterns can give an attractive effect. Be sure to buy a few spare tiles of each colour to replace damaged or worn areas later.

Above *Cork floor tiles are one of the most economic floor coverings available. They are easy to lay and can be easily extended to cover adjacent areas like this seating unit.*

Left *Rubber flooring was originally developed for commercial purposes but is now available for domestic use. It is very hard-wearing whilst being soft on the feet.*

Preparing Floors

If the floor is affected by damp, you should get professional advice. It can be difficult to be certain of the exact causes and building practices vary in different areas. When obtaining advice, be sure to state your intended floor covering to ensure it will be compatible with the remedy proposed. If you do the work yourself, read all manufacturers' recommendations on the products used. All solid floors must have a damp proof membrane.

Preparing for ceramic floor tiles

Concrete floors that are smooth, dry and flat are suitable for all types of tile and methods of laying. If the floor is new, it should be left for 4 weeks before any tiles are laid.

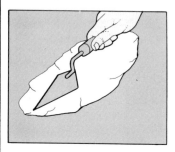

Any small holes or dips in the surface should be filled with a mix of 1 part cement to 3 parts sharp sand. Use a proprietary bonding agent (pva) in the mix, and brush the area to be filled with the bonding agent diluted with water immediately before filling.

Uneven concrete floors should be checked with a long batten

and spirit level to determine the difference in height between the highest and lowest point.

If this is not more than 12mm, you can use a self levelling screed compound.

Wire brush any dirt out of cracks and wash the entire floor with detergent and water to remove oil or grease.

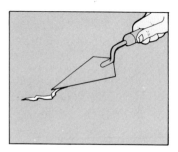

Fill all deep (10mm) cracks with 3 to 1 sand and cement morter, using a bonding agent, as above.

Mix up the self levelling compound according to the manufacturers' instructions. It should be a creamy consistency and have no lumps.

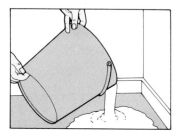

Starting in the furthest corner from the door, pour some on to the floor.

Spread it with a steel float to a depth of about 3mm. Don't worry about marks in the surface as these disappear as the compound levels itself.

Continue to pour and spread until you finish at the door.

Leave the compound to harden (see manufacturers' instructions). When the floor is hard enough to walk on, use a little water and the float to smooth any small bumps on the surface.

If the floor is too uneven to use a self levelling compound, the tiles will have to be laid on a *sand and cement screed* at least 12mm thick at the highest point of the floor. See the tile manufacturers' instructions concerning the minimum thickness.

You can choose to lay the screed first and leave it several weeks to harden before fixing the tiles with thin bed adhesive. However, tiles are best laid directly onto the new screed, so it is better to do the job all at once. (See page 24.)

The only preparation necessary before laying the screed is to give the floor a coat of proprietary sealer if the surface is dusty.

Old tiled floors may be tiled over, providing the tiles are securely fixed. Tap each one with a piece of wood to see if any sound 'hollow'. Any that

do need taking up and re-placing with adhesive, or the gap filled with sand and cement.

If you want to remove the old tiles, perhaps to keep the floor at the same level, use a bolster and club hammer at the base of each tile. Depending on how the tiles were fixed, you may have to use a self levelling screed on the floor beneath.

Wood Floors
Although concrete is the most suitable surface, you can use a special flexible adhesive to lay tiles on well prepared wood floors. The sand and cement screed method is not suitable.

Since you will need to line the floor with plywood or chipboard sheets, make sure that you won't need access to pipes or wiring under the floor. Also, as the tiled floor will be almost airtight, check that underfloor ventilation is adequate.

Parquet or wood block floors that are flat may be covered with 3mm thick hardboard instead.

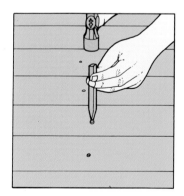

Drive the old nails below the surface and nail down loose boards.

Use plywood or chipboard at least 12mm thick. These are available in various sheet sizes, so work out the most economical ones to buy. Cut them to fit and put them in place.

Walk on the floor to check for movement. If necessary, insert packing underneath to level the edges where the sheets join.

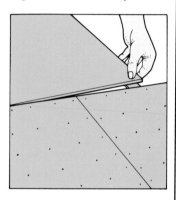

Drive nails every 10cm over the whole surface. Be sure to use nails of a length that won't go all the way through the floorboards beneath. They may penetrate pipes or wiring.

Once nailed down, the sheets must be sealed with two coats of oil based or water based primer.

Preparing for soft floor tiles

Follow the same procedure just described for each type of floor. The main consideration is the smoothness of the floor. Any small bumps or hollows will quickly show through the tiles and cause uneven wear.

If a sand and cement screed is necessary, it will have to be left approximately four weeks before being tiled.

Laying Floor Tiles

It is easier to set out floor tiles than wall tiles because you can dry lay them (ie: without adhesive). All floor tiles (except ceramic tiles being fixed on a fresh cement mortar screed) are laid from the centre of the room towards the edges. Therefore, the first job is to find the centre of the room.

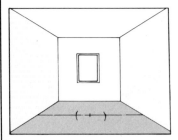

If the room is *square or rectangular*, measure two opposite walls and mark the centre of each. Then snap a chalk line between the two marks.

Measure and mark the centre of the chalk line and this is the centre of the room. Now you need a line at right angles to the first. Using a scriber (as described in 'Tools and Materials') place one nail on the centre mark and scratch a mark either side on the chalk line.

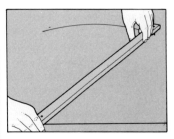

Place the nail on one of the scribed marks, and scribe an arc to both sides of the line.

Then repeat with the nail on the second mark.

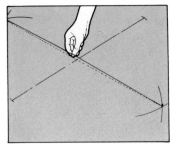

Snap a line between the points where the arcs intersect, and this line will be at right angles to the first line.

If the room is *not regular in shape*, it is usually best to set out the tiles parallel with the wall where the main entrance door is situated.

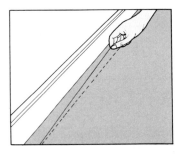

Measure 10cm from the wall at each side and snap a chalk line between the marks. Measure and mark the centre of the line.

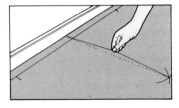

Use the scriber to mark the line either side of the centre and

then scribe arcs from each of these points. Snap a chalk line between the centre mark of the line and the point where the arcs intersect. The second line will be at right angles to the first. Extend across the floor.

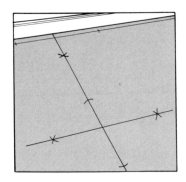

Measure the second line and mark its centre. Use the scriber as described above and snap a third line at right angles to the second one.

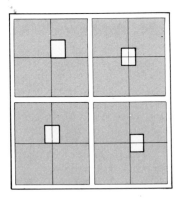

Once there are two central lines at right angles to each other, dry lay a row of tiles in both directions across the room. The first tile can be placed in any one of four positions where the lines intersect. Adjust the rows until there is at least $\frac{1}{2}$ a tile width left at the border on each side.

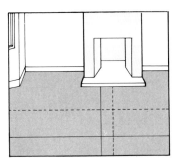

If the room has a major feature such as a fireplace or bay window, centre the tiles on it by snapping new chalk lines parallel to the old ones. Two features (on adjacent walls) are the most that can be treated this way. If in doubt as to what features to use, dry lay as many tiles as necessary to see which arrangement is best.

Laying ceramic tiles on thin bed adhesive

Set out the floor and dry lay the tiles as described above. Push the lugs of self spacing tiles together or, if there are no lugs, use a piece of cardboard or wood. The manufacturer of the tiles may recommend minimum joint gaps.

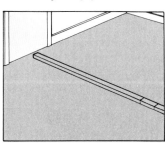

Fix a straight batten along the chalk line that is at right angles to the door and mark the position of the first (or central) tile.

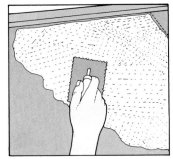

Spread about 1 square metre of adhesive with the notched trowel, making sure to get it up to the batten. Working on a small area makes sure the adhesive is wet enough when the tiles are laid. If you find that there is a skin forming on the surface, remove the adhesive and spread that area again.

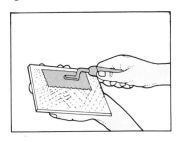

If the adhesive manufacturer recommends that the tiles (as well as the floor) should be 'buttered' with adhesive, follow the instructions as to thickness.

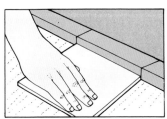

Lay the first tile at the mark and push each tile firmly into

the adhesive to create a good bond and eliminate air gaps.

If necessary, space the tiles with the same piece of cardboard or wood used when dry laying them.

Keep a close eye on the joins running at right angles to the batten to keep them straight.

Check every three or four rows with a batten for straightness, both along the edges and across the tops. Adjust, if necessary, before the adhesive has started to set.

Keep spreading areas of adhesive and laying tiles until all the whole tiles are laid, always working toward the door.

Remove adhesive from the edges of the floor where cut tiles will be laid.

Remove the batten carefully. Repeat on the other side of the room, working toward the door. Tile the rest of the floor.

When all the whole tiles are laid, leave the floor without walking on it for 24 hours (see manufacturers' instructions). If there must be some traffic (after several hours), place some sheets of plywood or similar to spread the load over a wide area.

Cutting ceramic floor tiles
You will need some type of heavy duty tile cutter for floor tiles. Hire shops usually have these and some tile stockists and contractors provide a cutting service. If you want to cut all the tiles before you start laying them, number each space and each tile on the back.

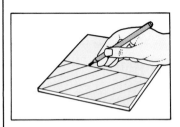

If you are taking the tiles away to be cut, mark the cutting lines with an indelible felt pen (or score with a spike on glazed tiles) and mark the waste side of the tile like this. Tiling

contractors use a circular saw with a thick blade that is cooled by water. They will need to cut on the waste side of the line, and pencil marks may get washed away.

Measure the tiles to be cut in the same way as wall tiles.

Grouting
Floor tiles are usually grouted with a mixture of cement and water. However, there are proprietary grouts and also coloured additives. Be sure to use a flexible grout on wooden subfloors. If you use these, follow the manufacturers' instructions for mixing. Otherwise, mix 1 part cement to 1 part water.

Pour some grout onto the tiles and use a rubber squeegee to push it well into the joints, pushing the excess to ungrouted areas. Work on an area you can reach without walking on the grout.

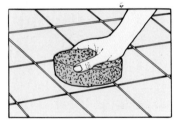

Wipe the surface of the tiles fairly clean with a damp

sponge. Don't worry about the thin film of grout that remains. This can be cleaned off later. Fill the joints with grout flush with the surface of the tiles, rather than using a rounded stick as with wall tiles.

Laying mosaics
This is best done on thin bed adhesive. It is possible to lay them on a sand and cement screed, but keeping them level is tricky. If your floor requires a screed, it's best to let it harden and use a self levelling compound if necessary. After a few weeks you can lay the mosaics with adhesive.

Set out and dry lay the sheets in the same way as floor tiles. Use a spacer of wood or card to make the gaps between the sheets the same as the gap between the individual chips.

Follow the same procedure as for ceramic floor tiles, and see the 'Mosaics' section of 'Tiling Walls' for methods of measuring the border sheets.

Cement mortar screed
To lay a level screed, you must work in bays formed by battens laid across the width of the room. Each bay must be set out, levelled, and filled with mortar. Then the mortar is tamped down, levelled off and the tiles are laid before moving to the next bay.

Begin by dry laying the tiles as for the adhesive method. As it won't be possible to use battens at right angles, you will have to keep the rows straight by eye. To help, you can stretch a string down the length of the room tied to nails driven into the skirting boards a few centimetres from the floor.

When you have found the best arrangement, mark the floor at the last row of full tiles at the furthest end of the room from the door and check that the line is square with the room. This will be the line of the first bay. Mark the skirting board at each end of the line to make it easy to position the first batten.

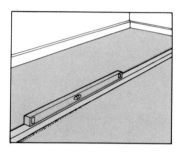

Use a long batten and spirit level to find the highest point on the floor. The screed will be 12mm thick (the thickness of the battens) at this point. The rest of the screed will be made level with this.

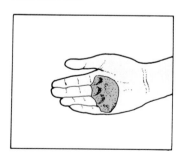

Prepare the mortar to the ratio of 3 parts sharp, washed sand to 1 part cement, mixing these thoroughly before adding water. Then mix only enough water to make the mortar hold its shape when squeezed in the hand; no more. This is called the semi dry method.

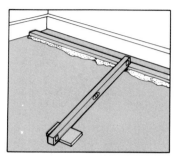

Place a piece of wood (or any object) 12mm thick on the highest part of the floor and lay the first batten of the bay on a layer of mortar. Use a batten and spirit level to level one end of the batten forming the bay to the highest point. Tamp the batten down or place more mortar under it to adjust it.

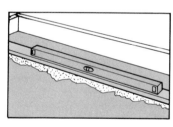

Then use the spirit level along the length of the batten to make it level with itself. Check that it is still on the line.

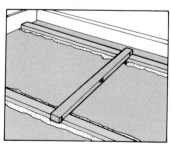

Next, lay the second batten on mortar parallel with the first, at a distance that you can reach

over easily, say 1 metre. Use the spirit level to make the second batten exactly level with the first along the entire length.

Shovel mortar into the bay, spreading it out with a float until the bay is filled above the level of the battens. Be careful not to knock the battens out of position.

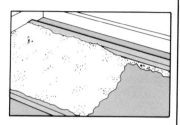

Tamp the mortar all over with the float, moving mortar from high spots to fill depressions. Keep adding and tamping until all the mortar is equally compressed.

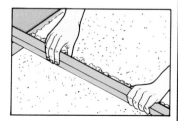

Use a straight batten to scrape the top of the mortar level with the battens. If necessary, tamp and scrape again until the entire bay is level.

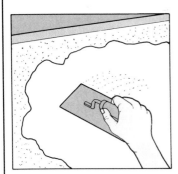

To help the tiles adhere to the screed, mix up a 'slurry' of 1 part cement to 1 part water and pour enough to cover the surface of the bay. Spread it over the screed with the float.

Lay the tiles, using a spacer card if necessary, starting with the back row. Tamp each one with the handle of the trowel to settle it firmly in the mortar.

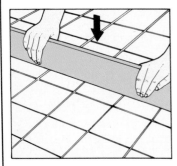

Use a timber straight edge to beat down all the tiles in the bay and then use the spirit level to check the tiles are flat.

When all the whole tiles are laid and levelled, you may cut the border tiles and lay them immediately. Otherwise you must use the trowel to remove a little mortar from the surface around the edges and cut and fix them later with thin bed adhesive. Be sure to leave enough depth for the edge tiles.

Lift the first batten carefully out of the mortar and place it in front of the second one to form the next bay. Repeat the levelling procedure and continue until the floor is finished.

Leave the floor without walking on it for 12 hours and then, when the border tiles are laid, grout all the tiles in the same way as for the adhesive method.

Cork, vinyl, rubber and carpet tiles

Set out the floor as for ceramic tiles, and fix a batten.

Use the adhesive recommended by the manufacturer. Cork tiles are usually fixed with a contact adhesive, and carpet, rubber and vinyl are usually fixed with a latex based flooring adhesive (unless they are self adhesive).

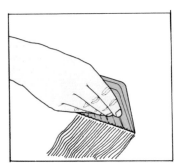

If you are using *flooring adhesive*, use a notched spreader to cover an area you can reach and begin laying the tiles immediately.

If you are using contact adhesive, spread an area you can reach and also coat the backs of enough tiles to cover the area, being careful not to let adhesive go over the edges. You will then have to follow the adhesive manufacturers' instructions about how long to wait before laying them.

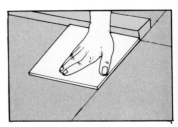

If the tiles are *self adhesive*, simply pull off the protective backing and stick them down.

through the bottom tile along the edge of the top tile.

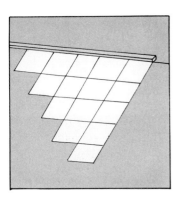

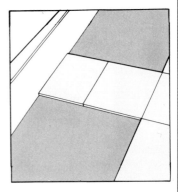

Lay the central tile first, and work outwards in both directions, filling in the middle spaces as you go.
· As you can walk on the newly laid tiles, it's possible to fill in the spaces around the edges immediately.

With these soft tiles, it is best to leave the last row of whole tiles until cutting the border tiles.

Simply reverse the position of the whole tile and the cut tile.

For fitting tiles around irregular shapes, follow the methods described for ceramic wall tiles, e.g. paper template etc. Cork, vinyl and rubber can be marked with a pencil, but a piece of chalk is best for carpet.

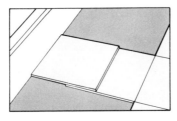

Dry lay a whole tile in the border space tight against the edge of an already fixed tile. This is the tile to be cut. Then place another whole tile on top with its edge touching the skirting board.

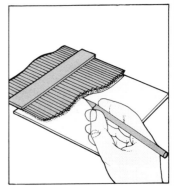

To position each tile, hold it above the floor with two edges against the battens (or the edges of previously laid tiles).´ This is especially important when using contact adhesive, as it may not be possible to adjust the tile once it's laid. Press each tile down firmly all over and use a damp cloth to wipe away any adhesive that is squeezed up between the edges.

Use a sharp knife (with replaceable blades) to cut

For rubber, vinyl and cork tiles, an adjustable shape tracing template can help when fitting around architraves and intricate shapes. A light placed directly above makes transferring the shape to the tile easier, simply trace the outline of the shadow.

SPECIAL EFFECTS

When laying tiles most of us don't think beyond a straight-forward covering of a single area with a chosen type of tile. Before making a final decision, consider if there are any individual touches that would set your job apart from others. Sometimes a clever use of contrasting or toning colours, or the introduction of some random tiles will put the designer stamp on it. Left-over tiles can be used for small areas such as table tops, decorative inserts in plasterwork, window ledges, etc, and so help to give a 'total' look to a room.

Above *Plain white and plain blue 100cm tiles completely cover this tiny modern bathroom. The blue abstract design on the cupboard door adds interest without interfering with the simplistic design.*

Right *A collection of antique tiles of different designs have been laid on this kitchen work top. If you decide to do this it is important to have a theme of one sort or another. It could be a question of colour, or subject perhaps, but there needs to be something to link that particular collection of odd tiles.*

Top left *A tessellated pattern of brown and white provencal tiles provides a softer line for this bedroom and adds some interest.*

Top right *Black and white vinyl tiles laid alternately in groups of four make this cheap form of floor covering look much more important. The fact that they have been laid diagonally across the room also helps.*

Left *Vinyl tiles come in many different colours, textures and patterns. Those covering the floor in this bathroom have been continued up the side of the bath, to match the decorative border design of the ceramic wall tiles. The border helps visually reduce the height of the room.*

TOP TEN TIPS

1. Estimating the number of tiles you need is quite simple. Because there are so many different sizes and shapes of tiles, it's best to calculate the area you're going to cover in square metres.

Tiles are usually sold in packs that state the area covered by each pack. This is usually 1–2 square metres for floor tiles and perhaps 2/3 square metre for wall tiles.

It's important to remember that you will need extra tiles to allow for breakages and other accidents during laying, so estimate generously. Also, it's always a good idea to have a few spares in case some are damaged in use. There can be colour variation in different batches of tiles, so it may not be possible to find matching ones later.

To find the area of a *floor*, simply multiply the length in metres by the width in metres. The result is the area in square metres.

If the room is irregular, find the area of alcoves and window bays separately. Then add these to the area of the main part of the floor.

In the same way, you can subtract the area of chimney breasts or cupboards where tiles won't be needed.

Finding the area of *walls* is done in the same way. Multiply the length of each wall by the height, and then subtract the areas of doors or windows. Once again, it is better to over estimate slightly.

Then, if you're estimating for *ceramic tiles* you must calculate the number of finished edge tiles to buy (either RE and REX or glazed edge universal).

As you may not know the size of the tiles you will choose, make a rough sketch showing the window or external corners where the edges need finishing. Write the length of these edges on the sketch.

When buying the tiles, substitute the finished edge tiles for field tiles. In other words, if you need 30 RE tiles for an external corner of two walls, buy 30 fewer field tiles than your original estimate.

Remember to allow extra finished edge tiles as well as field tiles.

The packaging of *adhesive* and *grout* always states the approximate area covered by the contents.

2. Resist the urge to begin fixing tiles as soon as you start work. Remember that the result depends most on the planning, so take your time setting out the job and the rest of the work will follow easily.

3. Here's how to remove and replace a damaged ceramic wall or floor tile.

Use a hammer to crack the tile into small pieces, starting from the centre and working outwards. Use only as much force as necessary. Chip out the pieces carefully with a narrow cold chisel and club hammer. Be careful not to damage the edge of the adjacent tiles.

When all the pieces are removed, chip away any adhesive and scrape away grout from the edges of the space. Vacuum out the dust and grit.

Dry lay the new tile to be sure it fits and that there is room beneath it for the adhesive.

Fix the tile and allow it to set before grouting.

4. To remove and replace a cork, rubber or vinyl tile, use an old wood chisel and a hammer.

Pierce the tile in the centre and work outwards, being careful not to lift the edges of adjacent tiles. Use a stiff scraping knife to remove the old adhesive, and vacuum the space well to be sure it's clean and free of debris. Now lay the new tile.

Apply the correct adhesive and bend the tile as you fit it into the space. It helps to warm vinyl tiles for a few minutes to make them more pliable.

Then press down firmly, from the centre toward the edges, to remove air bubbles.

5. To drill holes in ceramic tiles for fixing towel rails etc., you should use a slow speed electric drill and a masonry drill bit. Mark the position of the hole with a felt tip pen, and stick clear adhesive tape over the mark. This helps keep the drill bit from slipping off the mark as the hole is being started.

Use the drill at the lowest speed and apply only gentle pressure.

If you insert a plastic plug into the hole to take a screw, push the head of the plug completely through the tile, into the wall. That way there is no chance of cracking the tile when the screw is tightened.

6. Be sure to use the right tile and adhesive for the job. Wall tiles for walls and floor tiles for floors and work surfaces or anywhere strength may be needed.

Use heat resistant tiles, adhesive and grout on fireplaces and kitchen work surfaces. Also, on surfaces where food is prepared, make sure the tiles have a non lead glaze and that the grout is non toxic and non stain. Special kitchen work surface grout is available.

Use frost proof tiles, adhesive and grout on exterior walls, patios, steps etc.

Use water proof adhesive and grout on areas that are often wet, such as shower cubicle walls and floors.

Finally, for any surface that is slightly flexible, such as chipboard (particle board) lined walls, plywood panels or hardboard covered wood floors, you must always use a flexible wall or floor tile adhesive.

7. If the grout on wall tiles becomes stained, it may be possible to clean it by rubbing it gently with a pencil eraser.

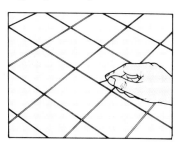

If the grout is too discoloured to be cleaned, use a nail to scrape out the old grout. Be careful not to damage the edges of the tiles.

Use a brush or vacuum cleaner to remove the dust and then regrout the tiles.

8. Where the edges of tiles meet a bath tub, sink or work surface, use silicone caulk instead of grout. This will remain flexible to absorb movement and resist staining. Make sure the gap to be filled is clean, dry and free of grease.

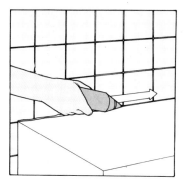

Apply the caulk direct from the nozzle of the tube, working in this direction.

Then smooth with a wet finger and remove any excess immediately with a damp cloth.

9. To fit quadrant tiles around a bath or basin, always work toward the centre of each wall from the ends.

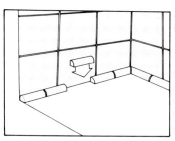

Fix the mitred tile in the corner and the round edge tile at the other end of the row. Then fix whole plain tiles until there is a gap left in the middle. Cut a plain tile to fit, leaving the correct gap either side.

10. When the tiling is finished, follow the manufacturers' instructions concerning sealing and maintenance.

Cork floor tiles must be sealed with polyurethane varnish unless they are ready sealed by the manufacturer.

Unglazed ceramic floor tiles and vinyl tiles must be sealed with the correct proprietary sealants recommended by the manufacturer.

Although rubber floor tiles are not usually sealed, some have a protective layer of wax that must be removed with a cloth dampened with white spirit (mineral spirits).

Safety Tips

When cutting tiles with a spike or trimming knife, make sure the tile is well supported and that all parts of your body are out of the way.

Wear gloves or use barrier cream to protect the skin of hands when working with cement, adhesives and grout.

Keep sharp tools, adhesives, grout and all products away from children and pets.

Don't wear a tie or loose clothing when using power tools.

Author
Dek Messecar
Series Consultant Editor
Bob Tattersall
Design
Mike Rose and Bob Lamb
Picture Research
Ann Lyons
Illustrations
Rob Shone, Rick Blakely

Dek Messecar is a professional joiner who has had experience on all aspects of DIY.

Bob Tattersall has been a DIY journalist for over 25 years and was editor of *Homemaker* for 16 years. He now works as a freelance journalist and broadcaster. Regular contact with the main DIY manufacturers keeps him up-to-date on all new products and developments. He has written many books on various aspects of DIY and, while he is considered 'an expert', he prefers to think of himself as a do-it-yourselfer who happens to be a journalist.

Photographs from Elizabeth Whiting Photo Library

Cover photography by Carl Warner
Materials for cover photograph supplied by Castlenau Tiles

The *Do It! Series* was conceived, edited and designed by Elizabeth Whiting & Associates and Robert Lamb & Company for William Collins Sons and Co Ltd

First published 1983
Reprinted 1983, 1985, 1986, 1987 (twice)

Revised edition first published 1989
9 8 7 6 5 4 3 2 1

Published by William Collins Sons & Co Ltd
London · Glasgow · Sydney · Auckland
Toronto · Johannesburg

ISBN 0 00 411896 0

Printed in Spain

Coordinador de la colección: Daniel Goldin
Diseño: Joaquín Sierra, sobre una maqueta
original de Juan Arroyo
Diseño de portada: Joaquín Sierra
Dirección artística: Mauricio Gómez Morín

A la orilla del viento...

Primera edición en alemán: 1995
Primera edición en español: 1997
Segunda reimpresión: 1999

Título original: *Die Schule fliegt ins Pfefferland*

© 1995, Benziger, Arena Verlag GmbH, Würzburg
ISBN 3-401-07136-X

D.R. © 1997, FONDO DE CULTURA ECONÓMICA
Av. Picacho Ajusco 227, México, 14200, D.F.

ISBN 968-16-5459-5
Impreso en México

EVELINE HASLER

ilustraciones de
JUAN GEDOVIUS

traducción de
ANA GARRALÓN

La escuela vuela

Atlanta International School
Ecole Internationale d'Atlanta
Colegio Internacional de Atlanta
International Schule Atlanta

FONDO DE CULTURA
ECONÓMICA

2890 NORTH FULTON DRIVE
ATLANTA, GEORGIA 30305

❖ A LEGUAS se veía que Andi nunca estaba contento.

—Este Andi es una cosa seria —decía a menudo su madre—. Cuando horneo un pastel de manzanas, él quiere un pastel de ciruelas. Cuando lo hago de ciruelas, se le antoja un bizcocho de chocolate. Lo que tiene, no lo quiere y lo que quiere, no lo tiene.

En la escuela, Nina, su compañera de asiento, a veces intentaba animarlo a jugar durante el recreo.

—Andi, ¿jugamos a la pelota? ¿O a saltar la cuerda? —le preguntaba.

Pero Andi sólo negaba con la cabeza.

—¡Déjalo! —decía la amiga de Nina. Y burlona le cantaba:

¡Como a Andi no le gusta nada,
mira todo con cara de col avinagrada!

Cuando se dirigía a la escuela Andi nunca se distraía. Siempre caminaba mirando fijamente delante de él. Jamás alzaba la vista ni saludaba a nadie.

Una mañana, en la parada del autobús, se topó con una anciana. Andi, claro está, nunca la había visto. Ella lo miró con sus ojillos entrecerrados y le dijo:

—Andi, es una lástima que siempre tengas esa cara de col avinagrada, no me gusta cómo luces, me acongojas. Me haría tan feliz que pudieras alegrarte como los demás niños, aunque fuera sólo una vez. Así que voy a hacer que hoy se te cumplan tres deseos. ¡Tan pronto como los pienses o los digas se realizarán! ¿Te agrada mi regalo?

Andi ni siquiera tuvo tiempo para sorprenderse. En ese momento sonaron ocho campanadas. Y se echó a correr para no llegar aún más tarde a la escuela.

Cuando entró al salón, la señora Schneider ya había repartido los cuadernos.

—Esta mañana tendremos dictado —dijo.

Eso a Andi no le gustó nada. Siempre se equivocaba en los dictados.

La profesora dictó:

—La hierba está mojada

Andi escribió:

—La sierba está enojada.

Ella dictó:

—Portentoso tiempo…

Andi escribió:

—Torpentoso lento…

—¡Andi, presta más atención! —le dijo la profesora al pasar junto a él.

Andi ya estaba enojado, pero con el regaño la cara se le puso más avinagrada.

"Qué escuela tan tonta", pensó, "¡ojalá se fuera al Congo!"

Apenas lo pensó, la escuela se

elevó suavemente. El edificio entero comenzó a flotar sin que nadie lo percibiera. Sólo Andi advirtió que las nubes pasaban extraordinariamente rápido.

El resto de los alumnos tenía la mirada concentrada en sus cuadernos,

De repente un leve temblor sacudió el aula. La escuela se había posado en algún lugar sobre la Tierra. La temperatura dentro del salón comenzó a aumentar con rapidez. Un suspiro quejumbroso recorrió las filas de asientos. En la primera fila, Max se quitó el suéter, pero siguió escribiendo sin distraerse.

—¡Uff!, este calor —dijo Nina. Miró hacia Andi y sacudió la sudorosa mano con la que escribía.

La profesora Schneider se pasaba la palma de la mano por la frente húmeda. Se le empapaban las palabras pero seguía dictando. Todavía con el libro en la mano abrió la ventana y, ahora sí, interrumpió el dictado. Estaba atónita: ¡donde antes crecían castaños, ahora había palmeras de grandes hojas que se

movían como abanicos tropicales!

La señora Schneider se frotó los ojos, luego se pellizcó y volvió a frotarse los ojos, pero las palmeras seguían ahí. De pronto pasó volando un papagayo y un mono saltó de una palmera.

Empapados en sudor, todos los niños miraron a la profesora. Afuera algo sucedía.

—Creo que estamos en África —alcanzó a decir Petra.

—Sí, ¡miren, qué palmeras tan altas! —exclamó Max, a quien le encantaba escalar—. ¡Apuesto a que puedo trepar y arrancar cocos para todos!

Enseguida salió corriendo del aula. La profesora todavía estaba pasmada y no dijo nada. Los demás lo siguieron y se arremolinaron a su alrededor.

Max revisó el tronco de la palmera con detenimiento.

—Es alto como un campanario. ¡Miren bien, en un segundo estoy arriba! —exclamó envalentonado. Se frotó las manos con saliva y comenzó a trepar.

Pero el tronco estaba muy resbaloso. Max avanzaba un poco y luego resbalaba.

—¡Tienes que subir, no bajar, fanfarrón! —gritó alguien.

Todos rieron.

Un par de niños lo animaron con una porra:

—¡Arriba, Max, arriba!

Andi observaba el paisaje. No podía creer lo que estaba pasando. De pronto alguien le tiró de la manga. Era Nina.

—Eh, Andi, algo se mueve entre los arbustos, me gustaría ver qué es. ¿A lo mejor encontramos nuevos amigos? Tengo curiosidad por

saber cómo son. ¿No quieres saber a qué juegan?

—*Mm* —dijo Andi—, pero si de veras
estamos en África, no sólo habrá gente amiga.
¡También nos podemos encontrar con animales
salvajes!

—¿Bestias feroces? —preguntó Nina asustada

—*Mm*, sí. Tigres, leones, leopardos —dijo Andi—. Aquí viven en libertad, no entre barrotes como en el zoológico.

Nina reflexionó un momento.

—¿De verdad crees que estemos en un lugar peligroso?

—Me temo que sí —dijo Andi—. Es mejor que investiguemos los dos juntos.

Andi y Nina miraron rápidamente hacia la señora Schneider. Estaba debajo de la palmera, con el rostro colorado y sudando como manguera. Miraba nerviosa hacia arriba.

—¡Max! ¿Me puedes escuchar? ¡Baja inmediatamente! —le gritó.

Todos estaban tan entretenidos que nadie se dio cuenta cuando Andi y Nina se alejaron.

Los dos iban muy juntos por un estrecho sendero que se internaba en la maleza.

Caminaron un buen rato. Detrás de los últimos matorrales vislumbraron una pequeña cabaña. Era toda redonda.

Afuera estaba una niña. Sostenía un platito y le daba de comer a unos pollos. Su piel era oscura y los cabellos eran de color negro azabache y crespos.

De pronto, la niña dejó el platito y comenzó a golpear un tambor: *dum, dum, dum*. Luego más rápido, cada vez mas rápido: *dum, dum, dum, dum...* En medio de un redoble se detuvo. Algo había llamado su atención. Miró fijamente hacia el sendero.

—No te muevas —susurró Nina y detuvo a Andi por el brazo

—Espero que no le demos miedo —le dijo—. A lo mejor nos toma por fantasmas.

Nina le sonrió a la niña.

Y ésta pareció perder su miedo. Sus ojos negros brillaban dulcemente. Entonces los niños se acercaron.

—Yo me llamo Nina
—dijo Nina y se señaló a sí
misma.

—Yo soy Andi —dijo
Andi. Con su dedo índice
se tocó el pecho.

La niña sonrió
abiertamente y dio un paso
adelante, se puso la mano
en el pecho y dijo:

—Limi, Limi.

Sonaba extraño. Pero
también bonito.

Nina sintió ganas de
tocar el tambor con la niña,
pero antes de que lo
alcanzara, Andi ya había
descubierto un río tras el
cañaveral.

—Hace tanto calor
—se quejó—. ¡Vamos a
nadar!

En la orilla del río se

sacó los zapatos. El agua se veía verde y misteriosa. Ramas y trozos de madera flotaban pesadamente en la corriente. Andi se internó en el agua. Apenas había dado unos pasos cuando escuchó un grito. Era Limi.

Su nueva amiga lo sujetó por el brazo. Con la otra mano señalaba al río.

Su dedo apuntaba hacia uno de los troncos flotantes. ¿Eran realmente eso? Andi miró con más cuidado: ¡No eran maderos!

—¡Mírales los ojos! —dijo sobresaltado.

Era cierto. De pronto uno de estos extraños troncos emergió del agua y abrió su gigantesca bocaza. Sobre la superficie relucía una fila de dientes puntiagudos.

Nina, que en ese momento también se había acercado a la orilla, alcanzó a decir

—¡Oh, caramba! Creo que son cocodrilos.
Mira ahí. Y ahí. Y allá también. Andi, por todos
lados nadan ojos.

—Y colmillos —añadió Andi. Su corazón latía
como el tambor de Limi. Pero Andi, en lugar de
agradecerle a Limi, empezó a protestar:

—¡Qué clase de lugar es éste! ¡Hace un calor
horrible y uno ni siquiera puede bañarse!

Disgustado, Andi metió el pie en uno de sus
zapatos.

—¡Ay! —gritó y lanzó el zapato lejos.

—¿Qué pasó? ¿Te mordió una serpiente?
—preguntó Nina más asustada.

Andi revisó su zapato: sólo se veían dos
hormigas.

—¡Son pequeñas, pero queman como el fuego!
—exclamó Andi. Saltaba en un pie.

Limi se rió.

—Claro, ¡son hormigas rojas! —dijo Nina—.
Las he visto en mi libro. Creo que son carnívoras.

"Esto ya es demasiado", pensó Andi
y comenzó a retornar por el sendero que los había
traído. Lo mejor era que volvieran con los demás.

Entre los matorrales no se veían los muros rojos de la escuela. Quizá la escuela ya había volado de regreso. ¿Qué tal que los hubieran abandonado a Nina y a él? Este pensamiento lo sobresaltó.

—¡Vamos, rápido! —apremió a Nina.

Los dos niños se despidieron de Limi con señas.

Limi con cara triste devolvió las señas. Su cabaña estaba apartada. Tal vez a ella le hubiera gustado conservar a Andi y a Nina como compañeros de juegos. Pero ellos estaban inquietos.

Después de una caminata agotadora llegaron nuevamente a la escuela. Andi respiró aliviado. No le hubiera gustado pasar la noche en ese territorio tan peligroso.

La señora Schneider, ya repuesta, había hecho regresar a los niños a la clase. Andi y Nina entraron los últimos.

La señora Schneider dijo:

—La disciplina es la disciplina. Siéntense bien y vuelvan a abrir sus cuadernos. ¡Me da igual donde esté nuestra escuela, tenemos que terminar el dictado!

Los niños se movieron sobre los cuadernos.

Afuera la algarabía de los papagayos era estridente. Casi no se entendía lo que dictaba la profesora. Ella tuvo que cerrar la ventana.

Andí tenía la mano empapada. Pero sus dedos se aferraban al lápiz.

—¡Este calor horroroso! —se quejó. Sin pensar demasiado, empezó a murmurar—: ¡Me gustaría que la escuela estuviera en el Polo Norte!

Apenas lo dijo, la escuela se elevó. Flotó tan suave e imperceptible que nadie en la clase se dio cuenta. La profesora dictaba de veras enojada y, otra vez, sólo Andi vio las nubes veloces.

Minutos más tarde, una tenue sacudida recorrió la clase: la escuela había aterrizado. Al instante los niños comenzaron a tiritar. Max en la primera fila volvió a ponerse su suéter.

En los vidrios de las ventanas se dibujaron

delgadas flores de hielo. La voz de la profesora se tornó afónica y temblorosa. De pronto interrumpió el dictado. Miró hacia afuera, abrió y cerró los ojos, se pellizcó y volvió a abrir y cerrar los ojos. Luego balbució:

—Esto sí que es increíble. Creo que nuestra escuela ha ido a parar al Polo Norte.

Acto seguido todos los niños corrieron hacia las ventanas.

Del techo colgaban carámbanos como heladas lanzas.

Nadie podía creerlo. Pero no había duda: la escuela se encontraba, como un barco naufragado, en un banco de hielo. A lo lejos se escuchaba el gruñido de un oso polar.

Max fue el primero en reaccionar:

—¡Vamos a construir un iglú! —dijo entusiasmado.

Pero la profesora exclamó:

—¡Qué estás diciendo! El aire está helado. ¡Sin guantes se te congelarán los dedos!

Nina interrumpió:

—¡Esperen! ¿No escuchan un ruido de

cascabeles a lo lejos? Son perros de trineo. Si los alcanzamos podríamos ir en el trineo. ¡Como bólidos sobre el hielo!

Los niños saltaron alborotados rumbo a la puerta. Pero la profesora, ya vuelta a sus cabales, dijo inflexible:

—Disciplina es disciplina. Esté donde esté nuestra escuela, el dictado debe terminarse.

Desilusionados, los niños volvieron a sentarse. Sus dedos entumecidos agarraron torpemente los lápices.

Al fondo del salón colgaba un reloj. También sus manecillas resintieron el frío y giraban lentamente. A la una y media se detuvieron. El dictado había terminado.

A Andi le empezaron a gruñir las tripas. De repente recordó la estancia de su casa y le entró nostalgia. Pero eso no ayudaba ahora que estaban en quién sabe qué parte del Polo Norte.

La estancia de su casa... ¡qué acogedora y agradable era en invierno! Al volver de la escuela casi siempre estaba la sopa en la mesa.

Su madre disponía de poco tiempo al

mediodía. Por la tarde ayudaba en la caja del supermercado.

Andi imaginó la sopa humeante y el suave olor de la cebada y el perejil.

Y, entre sus recuerdos, se le apareció su madre. Estaba de pie junto a la ventana y miraba hacia afuera. Estaba preocupada, como siempre que él llegaba tarde a casa. ¿Retornarían él y sus compañeros de clase a sus hogares?

"Me gustaría que nuestra escuela volviera a donde siempre ha estado, para que todos podamos regresar a casa."

Ése fue el tercer deseo de Andi.

Apenas lo pensó la escuela despegó. Voló imperceptiblemente a través de las nubes. Otra vez, sólo Andi pudo verlo. Instantes después aterrizó con una ligera sacudida.

Por la ventana aparecieron los verdes castaños del patio de la escuela. La profesora fue hacia la ventana. Suspiró aliviada.

—¡Menos mal que estamos de nuevo aquí! —les dijo a los niños—. Guarden sus cuadernos.

Los niños se agolparon en la puerta. Afuera se

percibía un ligero olor a salchichas y papas asadas.
Esta vez no miró el suelo como siempre lo
hacía. Andi miró con atención todo lo que estaba

a su alrededor en el camino a casa. Observó por primera vez lo bonitas que se veían las casas con sus balconcitos, las plantas y los letreros.

Un par de nubes alegraba el cielo azul por encima de los tejados. Nina caminaba contenta por la acera de enfrente.

—¡Adiós! —le dijo Andi con una gran sonrisa.

Nina volteó desconcertada. Por lo general Andi caminaba muy triste y no saludaba a nadie.

—¡Buen apetito! —dijo Andi—. ¿Quieres que paseemos en bicicleta juntos esta tarde?

Nina asintió.

En la parada del autobús Andi se encontró con la anciana que le había concedido los tres deseos por la mañana.

—Pareces contento, Andi. ¿Has deseado algo bueno?

Andi asintió.

—¿Se puede saber qué fue lo que deseaste? —preguntó la anciana señora.

Andi sonrió y dijo:

—He deseado que todo permanezca como está. ❖

Este libro se terminó de imprimir y encuadernar en el mes de mayo de 1999 en Impresora y Encuadernadora Progreso, S. A. de C. V. (IEPSA), Calz. de San Lorenzo, 244; 09830 México, D. F. Se tiraron 7 000 ejemplares.

J
F
HAS
Sp